FINISH LINE ACHIEVEMENTS
THE RUNNER'S ULTIMATE RACING JOURNAL

ROBIN GROVES

FINISH LINE ACHIEVEMENTS
THE RUNNER'S ULTIMATE RACING JOURNAL

ROBIN GROVES

www.finishlineachievements.com

First Edition

Proudly printed the United States of America on acid-free, archival-safe paper.

ISBN 978-0-9965912-0-1

Maps courtesy of Bruce Jones Inc. and FreeUSandWorldMaps.com

Included listing of specific companies, organizations, websites, etc. does not imply endorsement by the author, nor does it imply their endorsement of this book. Likewise, omission from the listing does not imply non-endorsement. Due of the dynamic nature of the internet, any websites listed may have changed since publication and may no longer be valid or current.

To Mike and Mitchell—

my personal and greatest running and race supporters.

To race directors who give us our finish lines,

volunteers who help us reach them,

supporters who cheer us on,

and fellow racers for the competition and inspiration

as we conquer each course and race the clock.

Contents

Introduction

We all know the same traits that make us successful, dedicated runners can make us equally devoted to recording and recalling our running statistics. Training journals or logs are perfect for recording our training data. This data can then be reviewed for specific training plans, injuries, clothing/shoe selections, mileage totals, and more, making a runner's personal training log an invaluable tool for learning from past experiences and building upon training successes.

If you are like me, you have a large collection of these annual training logs. Buried within their pages, amidst training weeks are countless race statistics and notes. Have you ever spent the night before a race searching endlessly through multiple training logs to try to find information from the same race that you ran who-knows-how-many years earlier? I'm sure that I am not the only one who has done that! Sometimes I wanted to find the name of the out-of-town restaurant we loved for a great post-race meal. Most often I was feverishly looking for my finish time, splits or PR for that particular race. Maybe you have kept, or have intended to keep, your race information in a notebook or on loose-leaf paper. Been there and done that, too! Though well-intentioned, it can lead to a lot of unstructured writing and inconsistent details. Some races are just unintentionally left out, and cross-referencing is practically impossible.

Finally, I had a "light bulb" moment—why not simply use a designated racing journal to record all of my race information within its pages?! There were so many training logs available; yet surprisingly, no race journals to be found. So, when you can't find what you are looking for, you just have to create it. Using my race-running experience and organizing skills, I set out to do just that.

Finish Line Achievements—The Runner's Ultimate Racing Journal is a comprehensive journal that has been specifically designed to make both documenting and reviewing personal race statistics quick, simple, and organized. Easy fill-in pages with top of the book (out of your way) binding, is friendly for use by both right-handed and left-handed racers. Personal race results can be referenced and cross-referenced by year, chronological order, specific race event, personal record, and distance. This will allow analysis of your statistics for comparison and for setting future race goals. While you may or may not use every section in this journal, use it flexibly to make it work for you. The more information that you record, the more knowledge you will easily be able to access, build from, and utilize. Record every serious statistic, every fun moment, or both. Begin to record your finish line achievements with current events and/or back-fill by compiling your previous race results.

Finish Line Achievements—The Runner's Ultimate Racing Journal has been thoughtfully planned and flexibly structured to be all-inclusive for racers (run, push rim, handcycle, walk) of every age, experience level, caliber and motivation—elite, front of the pack, middle of the pack, back of the pack, age-group/division competitive, recreational, social, relay, adventure, destination, and philanthropic; participating in road, path, track, cross country, or trail events. This book is for each of us who cross the start line and race to our own finish line achievements.

CROSSING THE START LINE REQUIRES COURAGE AND FAITH,

WHILE CROSSING THE FINISH LINE IS A PERSONAL DEMONSTRATION OF

DETERMINATION AND STRONG WILL.

THIS IS DOCUMENTED PROOF OF YOUR STRENGTH. THIS IS YOUR RACING LEGACY.

AS YOU CHASE DOWN YOUR DREAMS AND ACCOMPLISH THOSE GOALS,

RECORD IT ALL HERE, REFERENCE YOUR RESULTS, AND

CELEBRATE YOUR FINISH LINE ACHIEVEMENTS!

Results for _____

Dates from _____ to _____ Volume # _____

If found, please contact _____

First Race Photo(s)

Courage—First Race!

Race Name _____ Distance _____ Location _____

Chose this race _____ Motivation/Inspiration _____

Date _____ Time _____ Course Terrain _____

Temperature _____ Weather Conditions _____

Clothes/Shoes/Gear _____

Race Goals _____

Finish Time _____ Ave. Pace _____ Age _____ Division _____ Age-Grade _____ % = _____

Splits _____

Overall Place _____ / _____ Gender Pace _____ / _____ Division Place _____ / _____

Before the Race _____

During the Race _____

After the Race _____

Special Spectators/Supporters _____

Met _____ Ran With _____

Notes _____

_____

_____

_____

First Marathon Photo(s)

Determination—First Marathon!

Race Name _____ Marathon – 26.2 Miles!   Location _____

Chose this Race_____ Motivation/Inspiration _____

Date _____ Time _____ Course Terrain _____

Temperature _____ Weather Conditions _____

Clothes/Shoes/Gear _____

Race Goals _____

Finish Time _____ Ave. Pace _____ Age _____ Division _____ Age-Grade _____ % =_____

Splits _____

Overall Place _____ / _____ Gender Place _____ / _____ Division Place _____ / _____

Before the Race _____

During the Race _____

After the Race _____

Special Spectators/Supporters _____

Met _____ Ran With _____

Favorite Course Signs _____

Remember (course tips, stay, eat) _____

Notes _____

_____

Greatest Racing Achievements

Date	Race Name	Distance	Achievement	Ref. Pg.

Greatest Racing Achievements

Date	Race Name	Distance	Achievement	Ref. Pg.

Year at a Glance—Annual Summary of Race Results for Year _____

Date	Race Name	Distance	Finish Time	Pace	Place	Ref. Pg.

Year at a Glance—Annual Summary of Race Results for Year _____

Date	Race Name	Distance	Finish Time	Pace	Place	Ref. Pg.

Year at a Glance—Annual Summary of Race Results for Year _____

Date	Race Name	Distance	Finish Time	Pace	Place	Ref. Pg.

Year at a Glance—Annual Summary of Race Results for Year _____

Date	Race Name	Distance	Finish Time	Pace	Place	Ref. Pg.

Year at a Glance—Annual Summary of Race Results for Year _____

Date	Race Name	Distance	Finish Time	Pace	Place	Ref. Pg.

Year at a Glance—Annual Summary of Race Results for Year _____

Date	Race Name	Distance	Finish Time	Pace	Place	Ref. Pg.

Year at a Glance—Annual Summary of Race Results for Year _____

Date	Race Name	Distance	Finish Time	Pace	Place	Ref. Pg.

Year at a Glance—Annual Summary of Race Results for Year _____

Date	Race Name	Distance	Finish Time	Pace	Place	Ref. Pg.

Year at a Glance—Annual Summary of Race Results for Year _____

Date	Race Name	Distance	Finish Time	Pace	Place	Ref. Pg.

Year at a Glance—Annual Summary of Race Results for Year _____

Date	Race Name	Distance	Finish Time	Pace	Place	Ref. Pg.

(Example) **Detailed Race Result**

Race Name _Air Force Marathon Race (hat-trick)_ Distance _10K_ Location _WPAFB Dayton, OH_

Date _9/20/14_ Time _7:30 a.m._ Course Terrain _Paved roads with some hills. First 2 miles up, then down._

Temperature _60°→70°_ Weather Conditions _Sunny and calm, comfortable at start, then a little warm_

Clothes/Shoes/Gear _Usual race shorts, yellow singlet, cranberry Wave Riders, new 10K playlist_

Raced this Event _Annual favorite. Fun new hat-trick challenge_ Goals _1st in age group & finish time equal to age_

Finish Time _48:40_ Ave. Pace _7:50/mile_ Age _47_ Division _F 45-49_ Age-Grade _68.71% = 44:09_

Splits _7:51, 8:16 (uphill) =16:07, 7:23 (what goes up...) =23:31, 7:30 =31:02, 8:10 (side stitch) =39:13, 7:55 =47:05, 1:31_

Overall Place _62/1645_ Gender Place _10/992_ Division Place _1/113_

Training Plan _Best 10K Workout & Marathon Lite_ Gender Winning Time _39:17_ Division Winning Time _48:40_

Special Spectators/Supporters _Mike & Mitchell_

Met _Keith & Robert – Paralyzed Veterans of America Racing Team @ After-Party_ Ran With _____

Remember for Next Time _Take 1675, not surface streets, for no traffic. Side stitch same place on course as last year._

Notes _Woke up with very sore throat race morning. Concentrate on proper breathing after transition from downhill to flat section._

Can see the finish line @ mile 4, but still 2.2 miles to go – not favorite part of the course. Faster than last year (7 sec.). 5 time race

repeat; course PR this year! Finally made age group goal; still chasing time goal! Grabbed Gatorade and water at finish, changed to

singlet with Half Marathon bib already pinned on, and off to next race start. First hat-trick, and it was fun!

Detailed Race Result

Race Name _____ Distance _____ Location _____

Date _____ Time _____ Course Terrain _____

Temperature _____ Weather Conditions _____

Clothes/Shoes/Gear _____

Raced this Event _____ Goals _____

Finish Time _____ Ave. Pace _____ Age _____ Division _____ Age-Grade _____ % = _____

Splits _____

Overall Place _____ / _____ Gender Place _____ / _____ Division Place _____ / _____

Training Plan _____ Gender Winning Time _____ Division Winning Time _____

Special Spectators/Supporters _____

Met _____ Ran With _____

Remember for Next Time _____

Notes _____

_____

_____

_____

_____

Detailed Race Result

Race Name _____ Distance _____ Location _____

Date _____ Time _____ Course Terrain _____

Temperature _____ Weather Conditions _____

Clothes/Shoes/Gear _____

Raced this Event _____ Goals _____

Finish Time _____ Ave. Pace _____ Age _____ Division _____ Age-Grade _____ % = _____

Splits _____

Overall Place _____ / _____ Gender Place _____ / _____ Division Place _____ / _____

Training Plan _____ Gender Winning Time _____ Division Winning Time _____

Special Spectators/Supporters _____

Met _____ Ran With _____

Remember for Next Time _____

Notes _____

_____

_____

_____

_____

Detailed Race Result

Race Name _____ Distance _____ Location _____

Date _____ Time _____ Course Terrain _____

Temperature _____ Weather Conditions _____

Clothes/Shoes/Gear _____

Raced this Event _____ Goals _____

Finish Time _____ Ave. Pace _____ Age _____ Division _____ Age-Grade _____ % = _____

Splits _____

Overall Place _____ / _____ Gender Place _____ / _____ Division Place _____ / _____

Training Plan _____ Gender Winning Time _____ Division Winning Time _____

Special Spectators/Supporters _____

Met _____ Ran With _____

Remember for Next Time _____

Notes _____

_____

_____

_____

_____

Detailed Race Result

Race Name _____ Distance _____ Location _____

Date _____ Time _____ Course Terrain _____

Temperature _____ Weather Conditions _____

Clothes/Shoes/Gear _____

Raced this Event _____ Goals _____

Finish Time _____ Ave. Pace _____ Age _____ Division _____ Age-Grade _____ % = _____

Splits _____

Overall Place _____ / _____ Gender Place _____ / _____ Division Place _____ / _____

Training Plan _____ Gender Winning Time _____ Division Winning Time _____

Special Spectators/Supporters _____

Met _____ Ran With _____

Remember for Next Time _____

Notes _____

_____

_____

_____

_____

_____

Detailed Race Result

Race Name _____ Distance _____ Location _____

Date _____ Time _____ Course Terrain _____

Temperature _____ Weather Conditions _____

Clothes/Shoes/Gear _____

Raced this Event _____ Goals _____

Finish Time _____ Ave. Pace _____ Age _____ Division _____ Age-Grade _____ % = _____

Splits _____

Overall Place _____ / _____ Gender Place _____ / _____ Division Place _____ / _____

Training Plan _____ Gender Winning Time _____ Division Winning Time _____

Special Spectators/Supporters _____

Met _____ Ran With _____

Remember for Next Time _____

Notes _____

_____

_____

_____

_____

Detailed Race Result

Race Name _____ Distance _____ Location _____

Date _____ Time _____ Course Terrain _____

Temperature _____ Weather Conditions _____

Clothes/Shoes/Gear _____

Raced this Event _____ Goals _____

Finish Time _____ Ave. Pace _____ Age _____ Division _____ Age-Grade _____ % = _____

Splits _____

Overall Place _____ / _____ Gender Place _____ / _____ Division Place _____ / _____

Training Plan _____ Gender Winning Time _____ Division Winning Time _____

Special Spectators/Supporters _____

Met _____ Ran With _____

Remember for Next Time _____

Notes _____

_____

_____

_____

_____

Detailed Race Result

Race Name _____ Distance _____ Location _____

Date _____ Time _____ Course Terrain _____

Temperature _____ Weather Conditions _____

Clothes/Shoes/Gear _____

Raced this Event _____ Goals _____

Finish Time _____ Ave. Pace _____ Age _____ Division _____ Age-Grade _____ % = _____

Splits _____

Overall Place _____ / _____ Gender Place _____ / _____ Division Place _____ / _____

Training Plan _____ Gender Winning Time _____ Division Winning Time _____

Special Spectators/Supporters _____

Met _____ Ran With _____

Remember for Next Time _____

Notes _____

_____

_____

_____

_____

Detailed Race Result

Race Name _____ Distance _____ Location _____

Date _____ Time _____ Course Terrain _____

Temperature _____ Weather Conditions _____

Clothes/Shoes/Gear _____

Raced this Event _____ Goals _____

Finish Time _____ Ave. Pace _____ Age _____ Division _____ Age-Grade _____ % = _____

Splits _____

Overall Place _____ / _____ Gender Place _____ / _____ Division Place _____ /

Training Plan _____ Gender Winning Time _____ Division Winning Time _____

Special Spectators/Supporters _____

Met _____ Ran With _____

Remember for Next Time _____

Notes _____

_____

_____

_____

_____

Detailed Race Result

Race Name _____ Distance _____ Location _____

Date _____ Time _____ Course Terrain _____

Temperature _____ Weather Conditions _____

Clothes/Shoes/Gear _____

Raced this Event _____ Goals _____

Finish Time _____ Ave. Pace _____ Age _____ Division _____ Age-Grade _____ % = _____

Splits _____

Overall Place _____ / _____ Gender Place _____ / _____ Division Place _____ / _____

Training Plan _____ Gender Winning Time _____ Division Winning Time _____

Special Spectators/Supporters _____

Met _____ Ran With _____

Remember for Next Time _____

Notes _____

_____

_____

_____

_____

Detailed Race Result

Race Name _____ Distance _____ Location _____

Date _____ Time _____ Course Terrain _____

Temperature _____ Weather Conditions _____

Clothes/Shoes/Gear _____

Raced this Event _____ Goals _____

Finish Time _____ Ave. Pace _____ Age _____ Division _____ Age-Grade _____ % = _____

Splits _____

Overall Place _____ / _____ Gender Place _____ / _____ Division Place _____ / _____

Training Plan _____ Gender Winning Time _____ Division Winning Time _____

Special Spectators/Supporters _____

Met _____ Ran With _____

Remember for Next Time _____

Notes _____

_____

_____

_____

_____

Detailed Race Result

Race Name _____ Distance _____ Location _____

Date _____ Time _____ Course Terrain _____

Temperature _____ Weather Conditions _____

Clothes/Shoes/Gear _____

Raced this Event _____ Goals _____

Finish Time _____ Ave. Pace _____ Age _____ Division _____ Age-Grade _____ % = _____

Splits_____

Overall Place _____ / _____ Gender Place _____ / _____ Division Place _____ / _____

Training Plan _____ Gender Winning Time _____ Division Winning Time _____

Special Spectators/Supporters _____

Met _____ Ran With _____

Remember for Next Time _____

Notes _____

_____

_____

_____

_____

_____

Detailed Race Result

Race Name _____ Distance _____ Location _____

Date _____ Time _____ Course Terrain _____

Temperature _____ Weather Conditions _____

Clothes/Shoes/Gear _____

Raced this Event _____ Goals _____

Finish Time _____ Ave. Pace _____ Age _____ Division _____ Age-Grade _____ % = _____

Splits _____

Overall Place _____ / _____ Gender Place _____ / _____ Division Place _____ / _____

Training Plan _____ Gender Winning Time _____ Division Winning Time _____

Special Spectators/Supporters _____

Met _____ Ran With _____

Remember for Next Time _____

Notes _____

_____

_____

_____

_____

Detailed Race Result

Race Name _____ Distance _____ Location _____

Date _____ Time _____ Course Terrain _____

Temperature _____ Weather Conditions _____

Clothes/Shoes/Gear _____

Raced this Event _____ Goals _____

Finish Time _____ Ave. Pace _____ Age _____ Division _____ Age-Grade _____ % = _____

Splits_____

Overall Place _____ / _____ Gender Place _____ / _____ Division Place _____ / _____

Training Plan _____ Gender Winning Time _____ Division Winning Time _____

Special Spectators/Supporters _____

Met _____ Ran With _____

Remember for Next Time _____

Notes _____

_____

_____

_____

_____

_____

Detailed Race Result

Race Name _____ Distance _____ Location _____

Date _____ Time _____ Course Terrain _____

Temperature _____ Weather Conditions _____

Clothes/Shoes/Gear _____

Raced this Event _____ Goals _____

Finish Time _____ Ave. Pace _____ Age _____ Division _____ Age-Grade _____ % = _____

Splits _____

Overall Place _____ / _____ Gender Place _____ / _____ Division Place _____ / _____

Training Plan _____ Gender Winning Time _____ Division Winning Time _____

Special Spectators/Supporters _____

Met _____ Ran With _____

Remember for Next Time _____

Notes _____

_____

_____

_____

_____

_____

Detailed Race Result

Race Name _____ Distance _____ Location _____

Date _____ Time _____ Course Terrain _____

Temperature _____ Weather Conditions _____

Clothes/Shoes/Gear _____

Raced this Event _____ Goals _____

Finish Time _____ Ave. Pace _____ Age _____ Division _____ Age-Grade _____ % = _____

Splits _____

Overall Place _____ / _____ Gender Place _____ / _____ Division Place _____ / _____

Training Plan _____ Gender Winning Time _____ Division Winning Time _____

Special Spectators/Supporters _____

Met _____ Ran With _____

Remember for Next Time _____

Notes _____

_____

_____

_____

_____

Detailed Race Result

Race Name _____ Distance _____ Location _____

Date _____ Time _____ Course Terrain _____

Temperature _____ Weather Conditions _____

Clothes/Shoes/Gear _____

Raced this Event _____ Goals _____

Finish Time _____ Ave. Pace _____ Age _____ Division _____ Age-Grade _____ % = _____

Splits _____

Overall Place _____ / _____ Gender Place _____ / _____ Division Place _____ / _____

Training Plan _____ Gender Winning Time _____ Division Winning Time _____

Special Spectators/Supporters _____

Met _____ Ran With _____

Remember for Next Time _____

Notes _____

_____

_____

_____

_____

Detailed Race Result

Race Name _____ Distance _____ Location _____

Date _____ Time _____ Course Terrain _____

Temperature _____ Weather Conditions _____

Clothes/Shoes/Gear _____

Raced this Event _____ Goals _____

Finish Time _____ Ave. Pace _____ Age _____ Division _____ Age-Grade _____ % = _____

Splits _____

Overall Place _____/_____ Gender Place _____/_____ Division Place _____/_____

Training Plan _____ Gender Winning Time _____ Division Winning Time _____

Special Spectators/Supporters _____

Met _____ Ran With _____

Remember for Next Time _____

Notes _____

_____

_____

_____

_____

Detailed Race Result

Race Name _____ Distance _____ Location _____

Date _____ Time _____ Course Terrain _____

Temperature _____ Weather Conditions _____

Clothes/Shoes/Gear _____

Raced this Event _____ Goals _____

Finish Time _____ Ave. Pace _____ Age _____ Division _____ Age-Grade _____ % = _____

Splits _____

Overall Place _____ / _____ Gender Place _____ / _____ Division Place _____ / _____

Training Plan _____ Gender Winning Time _____ Division Winning Time _____

Special Spectators/Supporters _____

Met _____ Ran With _____

Remember for Next Time _____

Notes _____

_____

_____

_____

_____

Detailed Race Result

Race Name _____ Distance _____ Location _____

Date _____ Time _____ Course Terrain _____

Temperature _____ Weather Conditions _____

Clothes/Shoes/Gear _____

Raced this Event _____ Goals _____

Finish Time _____ Ave. Pace _____ Age _____ Division _____ Age-Grade _____ % = _____

Splits _____

Overall Place _____ / _____ Gender Place _____ / _____ Division Place _____ / _____

Training Plan _____ Gender Winning Time _____ Division Winning Time _____

Special Spectators/Supporters _____

Met _____ Ran With _____

Remember for Next Time _____

Notes _____

_____

_____

_____

_____

Detailed Race Result

Race Name _____ Distance _____ Location _____

Date _____ Time _____ Course Terrain _____

Temperature _____ Weather Conditions _____

Clothes/Shoes/Gear _____

Raced this Event _____ Goals _____

Finish Time _____ Ave. Pace _____ Age _____ Division _____ Age-Grade _____ % = _____

Splits _____

Overall Place _____ / _____ Gender Place _____ / _____ Division Place _____ / _____

Training Plan _____ Gender Winning Time _____ Division Winning Time _____

Special Spectators/Supporters _____

Met _____ Ran With _____

Remember for Next Time _____

Notes _____

_____

_____

_____

_____

Detailed Race Result

Race Name _____ Distance _____ Location _____

Date _____ Time _____ Course Terrain _____

Temperature _____ Weather Conditions _____

Clothes/Shoes/Gear _____

Raced this Event _____ Goals _____

Finish Time _____ Ave. Pace _____ Age _____ Division _____ Age-Grade _____ % = _____

Splits _____

Overall Place _____ / _____ Gender Place _____ / _____ Division Place _____ / _____

Training Plan _____ Gender Winning Time _____ Division Winning Time _____

Special Spectators/Supporters _____

Met _____ Ran With _____

Remember for Next Time _____

Notes _____

_____

_____

_____

_____

Detailed Race Result

Race Name _____ Distance _____ Location _____

Date _____ Time _____ Course Terrain _____

Temperature _____ Weather Conditions _____

Clothes/Shoes/Gear _____

Raced this Event _____ Goals _____

Finish Time _____ Ave. Pace _____ Age _____ Division _____ Age-Grade _____ % = _____

Splits _____

Overall Place _____ / _____ Gender Place _____ / _____ Division Place _____ / _____

Training Plan _____ Gender Winning Time _____ Division Winning Time _____

Special Spectators/Supporters _____

Met _____ Ran With _____

Remember for Next Time _____

Notes _____

_____

_____

_____

_____

Detailed Race Result

Race Name _____ Distance _____ Location _____

Date _____ Time _____ Course Terrain _____

Temperature _____ Weather Conditions _____

Clothes/Shoes/Gear _____

Raced this Event _____ Goals _____

Finish Time _____ Ave. Pace _____ Age _____ Division _____ Age-Grade _____ % = _____

Splits _____

Overall Place _____ / _____ Gender Place _____ / _____ Division Place _____ / _____

Training Plan _____ Gender Winning Time _____ Division Winning Time _____

Special Spectators/Supporters _____

Met _____ Ran With _____

Remember for Next Time _____

Notes _____

_____

_____

_____

_____

_____

Detailed Race Result

Race Name _____ Distance _____ Location _____

Date _____ Time _____ Course Terrain _____

Temperature _____ Weather Conditions _____

Clothes/Shoes/Gear _____

Raced this Event _____ Goals _____

Finish Time _____ Ave. Pace _____ Age _____ Division _____ Age-Grade _____ % = _____

Splits _____

Overall Place _____ / _____ Gender Place _____ / _____ Division Place _____ / _____

Training Plan _____ Gender Winning Time _____ Division Winning Time _____

Special Spectators/Supporters _____

Met _____ Ran With _____

Remember for Next Time _____

Notes _____

_____

_____

_____

_____

Detailed Race Result

Race Name _____ Distance _____ Location _____

Date _____ Time _____ Course Terrain _____

Temperature _____ Weather Conditions _____

Clothes/Shoes/Gear _____

Raced this Event _____ Goals _____

Finish Time _____ Ave. Pace _____ Age _____ Division _____ Age-Grade _____ % = _____

Splits _____

Overall Place _____ / _____ Gender Place _____ / _____ Division Place _____ / _____

Training Plan _____ Gender Winning Time _____ Division Winning Time _____

Special Spectators/Supporters _____

Met _____ Ran With _____

Remember for Next Time _____

Notes _____

_____

_____

_____

_____

_____

Detailed Race Result

Race Name _____ Distance _____ Location _____

Date _____ Time _____ Course Terrain _____

Temperature _____ Weather Conditions _____

Clothes/Shoes/Gear _____

Raced this Event _____ Goals _____

Finish Time _____ Ave. Pace _____ Age _____ Division _____ Age-Grade _____ % = _____

Splits _____

Overall Place _____ / _____ Gender Place _____ / _____ Division Place _____ / _____

Training Plan _____ Gender Winning Time _____ Division Winning Time _____

Special Spectators/Supporters _____

Met _____ Ran With _____

Remember for Next Time _____

Notes _____

_____

_____

_____

_____

Detailed Race Result

Race Name _____ Distance _____ Location _____

Date _____ Time _____ Course Terrain _____

Temperature _____ Weather Conditions _____

Clothes/Shoes/Gear _____

Raced this Event _____ Goals _____

Finish Time _____ Ave. Pace _____ Age _____ Division _____ Age-Grade _____ % = _____

Splits _____

Overall Place _____ / _____ Gender Place _____ / _____ Division Place _____ / _____

Training Plan _____ Gender Winning Time _____ Division Winning Time _____

Special Spectators/Supporters _____

Met _____ Ran With _____

Remember for Next Time _____

Notes _____

_____

_____

_____

_____

Detailed Race Result

Race Name _____ Distance _____ Location _____

Date _____ Time _____ Course Terrain _____

Temperature _____ Weather Conditions _____

Clothes/Shoes/Gear _____

Raced this Event _____ Goals _____

Finish Time _____ Ave. Pace _____ Age _____ Division _____ Age-Grade _____ % = _____

Splits _____

Overall Place _____ / _____ Gender Place _____ / _____ Division Place _____ / _____

Training Plan _____ Gender Winning Time _____ Division Winning Time _____

Special Spectators/Supporters _____

Met _____ Ran With _____

Remember for Next Time _____

Notes _____

_____

_____

_____

_____

Detailed Race Result

Race Name _____ Distance _____ Location _____

Date _____ Time _____ Course Terrain _____

Temperature _____ Weather Conditions _____

Clothes/Shoes/Gear _____

Raced this Event _____ Goals _____

Finish Time _____ Ave. Pace _____ Age _____ Division _____ Age-Grade _____ % = _____

Splits _____

Overall Place _____ / _____ Gender Place _____ / _____ Division Place _____ / _____

Training Plan _____ Gender Winning Time _____ Division Winning Time _____

Special Spectators/Supporters _____

Met _____ Ran With _____

Remember for Next Time _____

Notes _____

_____

_____

_____

_____

_____

Detailed Race Result

Race Name _____ Distance _____ Location _____

Date _____ Time _____ Course Terrain _____

Temperature _____ Weather Conditions _____

Clothes/Shoes/Gear _____

Raced this Event _____ Goals _____

Finish Time _____ Ave. Pace _____ Age _____ Division _____ Age-Grade _____ % = _____

Splits _____

Overall Place _____ / _____ Gender Place _____ / _____ Division Place _____ / _____

Training Plan _____ Gender Winning Time _____ Division Winning Time _____

Special Spectators/Supporters _____

Met _____ Ran With _____

Remember for Next Time _____

Notes _____

_____

_____

_____

_____

Detailed Race Result

Race Name _____ Distance _____ Location _____

Date _____ Time _____ Course Terrain _____

Temperature _____ Weather Conditions _____

Clothes/Shoes/Gear _____

Raced this Event _____ Goals _____

Finish Time _____ Ave. Pace _____ Age _____ Division _____ Age-Grade _____ % = _____

Splits _____

Overall Place _____ / _____ Gender Place _____ / _____ Division Place _____ /

Training Plan _____ Gender Winning Time _____ Division Winning Time _____

Special Spectators/Supporters _____

Met _____ Ran With _____

Remember for Next Time _____

Notes _____

_____

_____

_____

_____

Detailed Race Result

Race Name _____ Distance _____ Location _____

Date _____ Time _____ Course Terrain _____

Temperature _____ Weather Conditions _____

Clothes/Shoes/Gear _____

Raced this Event _____ Goals _____

Finish Time _____ Ave. Pace _____ Age _____ Division _____ Age-Grade _____ % = _____

Splits _____

Overall Place _____ / _____ Gender Place _____ / _____ Division Place _____ / _____

Training Plan _____ Gender Winning Time _____ Division Winning Time _____

Special Spectators/Supporters _____

Met _____ Ran With _____

Remember for Next Time _____

Notes _____

_____

_____

_____

_____

_____

Detailed Race Result

Race Name _____ Distance _____ Location _____

Date _____ Time _____ Course Terrain _____

Temperature _____ Weather Conditions _____

Clothes/Shoes/Gear _____

Raced this Event _____ Goals _____

Finish Time _____ Ave. Pace _____ Age _____ Division _____ Age-Grade _____ % =

Splits _____

Overall Place _____ / _____ Gender Place _____ / _____ Division Place _____ /

Training Plan _____ Gender Winning Time _____ Division Winning Time _____

Special Spectators/Supporters _____

Met _____ Ran With _____

Remember for Next Time _____

Notes _____

_____

_____

_____

_____

Detailed Race Result

Race Name _____ Distance _____ Location _____

Date _____ Time _____ Course Terrain _____

Temperature _____ Weather Conditions _____

Clothes/Shoes/Gear _____

Raced this Event _____ Goals _____

Finish Time _____ Ave. Pace _____ Age _____ Division _____ Age-Grade _____ % = _____

Splits _____

Overall Place _____ / _____ Gender Place _____ / _____ Division Place _____ / _____

Training Plan _____ Gender Winning Time _____ Division Winning Time _____

Special Spectators/Supporters _____

Met _____ Ran With _____

Remember for Next Time _____

Notes _____

_____

_____

_____

_____

_____

Detailed Race Result

Race Name _____ Distance _____ Location _____

Date _____ Time _____ Course Terrain _____

Temperature _____ Weather Conditions _____

Clothes/Shoes/Gear _____

Raced this Event _____ Goals _____

Finish Time _____ Ave. Pace _____ Age _____ Division _____ Age-Grade _____ % = _____

Splits _____

Overall Place _____ / _____ Gender Place _____ / _____ Division Place _____ / _____

Training Plan _____ Gender Winning Time _____ Division Winning Time _____

Special Spectators/Supporters _____

Met _____ Ran With _____

Remember for Next Time _____

Notes _____

_____

_____

_____

_____

Detailed Race Result

Race Name _____ Distance _____ Location _____

Date _____ Time _____ Course Terrain _____

Temperature _____ Weather Conditions _____

Clothes/Shoes/Gear _____

Raced this Event _____ Goals _____

Finish Time _____ Ave. Pace _____ Age _____ Division _____ Age-Grade _____ % = _____

Splits _____

Overall Place _____ / _____ Gender Place _____ / _____ Division Place _____ / _____

Training Plan _____ Gender Winning Time _____ Division Winning Time _____

Special Spectators/Supporters _____

Met _____ Ran With _____

Remember for Next Time _____

Notes _____

_____

_____

_____

_____

Detailed Race Result

Race Name _____ Distance _____ Location _____

Date _____ Time _____ Course Terrain _____

Temperature _____ Weather Conditions _____

Clothes/Shoes/Gear _____

Raced this Event _____ Goals _____

Finish Time _____ Ave. Pace _____ Age _____ Division _____ Age-Grade _____ % = _____

Splits _____

Overall Place _____ / _____ Gender Place _____ / _____ Division Place _____ / _____

Training Plan _____ Gender Winning Time _____ Division Winning Time _____

Special Spectators/Supporters _____

Met _____ Ran With _____

Remember for Next Time _____

Notes _____

_____

_____

_____

_____

Detailed Race Result

Race Name _____ Distance _____ Location _____

Date _____ Time _____ Course Terrain _____

Temperature _____ Weather Conditions _____

Clothes/Shoes/Gear _____

Raced this Event _____ Goals _____

Finish Time _____ Ave. Pace _____ Age _____ Division _____ Age-Grade _____ % = _____

Splits _____

Overall Place _____ / _____ Gender Place _____ / _____ Division Place _____ / _____

Training Plan _____ Gender Winning Time _____ Division Winning Time _____

Special Spectators/Supporters _____

Met _____ Ran With _____

Remember for Next Time _____

Notes _____

_____

_____

_____

_____

_____

Detailed Race Result

Race Name _____ Distance _____ Location _____

Date _____ Time _____ Course Terrain _____

Temperature _____ Weather Conditions _____

Clothes/Shoes/Gear _____

Raced this Event _____ Goals _____

Finish Time _____ Ave. Pace _____ Age _____ Division _____ Age-Grade _____ % = _____

Splits _____

Overall Place _____ / _____ Gender Place _____ / _____ Division Place _____ / _____

Training Plan _____ Gender Winning Time _____ Division Winning Time _____

Special Spectators/Supporters _____

Met _____ Ran With _____

Remember for Next Time _____

Notes _____

_____

_____

_____

_____

_____

Detailed Race Result

Race Name _____ Distance _____ Location _____

Date _____ Time _____ Course Terrain _____

Temperature _____ Weather Conditions _____

Clothes/Shoes/Gear _____

Raced this Event _____ Goals _____

Finish Time _____ Ave. Pace _____ Age _____ Division _____ Age-Grade _____ % = _____

Splits _____

Overall Place _____ / _____ Gender Place _____ / _____ Division Place _____ / _____

Training Plan _____ Gender Winning Time _____ Division Winning Time _____

Special Spectators/Supporters _____

Met _____ Ran With _____

Remember for Next Time _____

Notes _____

_____

_____

_____

_____

_____

Detailed Race Result

Race Name _____ Distance _____ Location _____

Date _____ Time _____ Course Terrain _____

Temperature _____ Weather Conditions _____

Clothes/Shoes/Gear _____

Raced this Event _____ Goals _____

Finish Time _____ Ave. Pace _____ Age _____ Division _____ Age-Grade _____ % = _____

Splits _____

Overall Place _____ / _____ Gender Place _____ / _____ Division Place _____ / _____

Training Plan _____ Gender Winning Time _____ Division Winning Time _____

Special Spectators/Supporters _____

Met _____ Ran With _____

Remember for Next Time _____

Notes _____

_____

_____

_____

_____

Detailed Race Result

Race Name _____ Distance _____ Location _____

Date _____ Time _____ Course Terrain _____

Temperature _____ Weather Conditions _____

Clothes/Shoes/Gear _____

Raced this Event _____ Goals _____

Finish Time _____ Ave. Pace _____ Age _____ Division _____ Age-Grade _____ % = _____

Splits _____

Overall Place _____ / _____ Gender Place _____ / _____ Division Place _____ / _____

Training Plan _____ Gender Winning Time _____ Division Winning Time _____

Special Spectators/Supporters _____

Met _____ Ran With _____

Remember for Next Time _____

Notes _____

_____

_____

_____

_____

Detailed Race Result

Race Name _____ Distance _____ Location _____

Date _____ Time _____ Course Terrain _____

Temperature _____ Weather Conditions _____

Clothes/Shoes/Gear _____

Raced this Event _____ Goals _____

Finish Time _____ Ave. Pace _____ Age _____ Division _____ Age-Grade _____ % = _____

Splits _____

Overall Place _____ / _____ Gender Place _____ / _____ Division Place _____ / _____

Training Plan _____ Gender Winning Time _____ Division Winning Time _____

Special Spectators/Supporters _____

Met _____ Ran With _____

Remember for Next Time _____

Notes _____

_____

_____

_____

_____

_____

Detailed Race Result

Race Name _____ Distance _____ Location _____

Date _____ Time _____ Course Terrain _____

Temperature _____ Weather Conditions _____

Clothes/Shoes/Gear _____

Raced this Event _____ Goals _____

Finish Time _____ Ave. Pace _____ Age _____ Division _____ Age-Grade _____ % = _____

Splits _____

Overall Place _____ / _____ Gender Place _____ / _____ Division Place _____ / _____

Training Plan _____ Gender Winning Time _____ Division Winning Time _____

Special Spectators/Supporters _____

Met _____ Ran With _____

Remember for Next Time _____

Notes _____

_____

_____

_____

_____

_____

Detailed Race Result

Race Name _____ Distance _____ Location _____

Date _____ Time _____ Course Terrain _____

Temperature _____ Weather Conditions _____

Clothes/Shoes/Gear _____

Raced this Event _____ Goals _____

Finish Time _____ Ave. Pace _____ Age _____ Division _____ Age-Grade _____ % = _____

Splits _____

Overall Place _____ / _____ Gender Place _____ / _____ Division Place _____ / _____

Training Plan _____ Gender Winning Time _____ Division Winning Time _____

Special Spectators/Supporters _____

Met _____ Ran With _____

Remember for Next Time _____

Notes _____

_____

_____

_____

_____

Detailed Race Result

Race Name _____ Distance _____ Location _____

Date _____ Time _____ Course Terrain _____

Temperature _____ Weather Conditions _____

Clothes/Shoes/Gear _____

Raced this Event _____ Goals _____

Finish Time _____ Ave. Pace _____ Age _____ Division _____ Age-Grade _____ % = _____

Splits _____

Overall Place _____ / _____ Gender Place _____ / _____ Division Place _____ / _____

Training Plan _____ Gender Winning Time _____ Division Winning Time _____

Special Spectators/Supporters _____

Met _____ Ran With _____

Remember for Next Time _____

Notes _____

_____

_____

_____

_____

_____

Detailed Race Result

Race Name _____ Distance _____ Location _____

Date _____ Time _____ Course Terrain _____

Temperature _____ Weather Conditions _____

Clothes/Shoes/Gear _____

Raced this Event _____ Goals _____

Finish Time _____ Ave. Pace _____ Age _____ Division _____ Age-Grade _____ % = _____

Splits_____

Overall Place _____ / _____ Gender Place _____ / _____ Division Place _____ / _____

Training Plan _____ Gender Winning Time _____ Division Winning Time _____

Special Spectators/Supporters _____

Met _____ Ran With _____

Remember for Next Time _____

Notes _____

_____

_____

_____

_____

_____

Detailed Race Result

Race Name _____ Distance _____ Location _____

Date _____ Time _____ Course Terrain _____

Temperature _____ Weather Conditions _____

Clothes/Shoes/Gear _____

Raced this Event _____ Goals _____

Finish Time _____ Ave. Pace _____ Age _____ Division _____ Age-Grade _____ % = ____

Splits _____

Overall Place _____ / _____ Gender Place _____ / _____ Division Place _____ / ____

Training Plan _____ Gender Winning Time _____ Division Winning Time _____

Special Spectators/Supporters _____

Met _____ Ran With _____

Remember for Next Time _____

Notes _____

_____

_____

_____

_____

Detailed Race Result

Race Name _____ Distance _____ Location _____

Date _____ Time _____ Course Terrain _____

Temperature _____ Weather Conditions _____

Clothes/Shoes/Gear _____

Raced this Event _____ Goals _____

Finish Time _____ Ave. Pace _____ Age _____ Division _____ Age-Grade _____ % = _____

Splits _____

Overall Place _____/_____ Gender Place _____/_____ Division Place _____/_____

Training Plan _____ Gender Winning Time _____ Division Winning Time _____

Special Spectators/Supporters _____

Met _____ Ran With _____

Remember for Next Time _____

Notes _____

_____

_____

_____

_____

Detailed Race Result

Race Name _____ Distance _____ Location _____

Date _____ Time _____ Course Terrain _____

Temperature _____ Weather Conditions _____

Clothes/Shoes/Gear _____

Raced this Event _____ Goals _____

Finish Time _____ Ave. Pace _____ Age _____ Division _____ Age-Grade _____ % = _____

Splits _____

Overall Place _____ / _____ Gender Place _____ / _____ Division Place _____ / _____

Training Plan _____ Gender Winning Time _____ Division Winning Time _____

Special Spectators/Supporters _____

Met _____ Ran With _____

Remember for Next Time _____

Notes _____

_____

_____

_____

_____

Detailed Race Result

Race Name _____ Distance _____ Location _____

Date _____ Time _____ Course Terrain _____

Temperature _____ Weather Conditions _____

Clothes/Shoes/Gear _____

Raced this Event _____ Goals _____

Finish Time _____ Ave. Pace _____ Age _____ Division _____ Age-Grade _____ % = _____

Splits _____

Overall Place _____ / _____ Gender Place _____ / _____ Division Place _____ / _____

Training Plan _____ Gender Winning Time _____ Division Winning Time _____

Special Spectators/Supporters _____

Met _____ Ran With _____

Remember for Next Time _____

Notes _____

_____

_____

_____

_____

_____

Detailed Race Result

Race Name _____ Distance _____ Location _____

Date _____ Time _____ Course Terrain _____

Temperature _____ Weather Conditions _____

Clothes/Shoes/Gear _____

Raced this Event _____ Goals _____

Finish Time _____ Ave. Pace _____ Age _____ Division _____ Age-Grade _____ % = _____

Splits _____

Overall Place _____ / _____ Gender Place _____ / _____ Division Place _____ / _____

Training Plan _____ Gender Winning Time _____ Division Winning Time _____

Special Spectators/Supporters _____

Met _____ Ran With _____

Remember for Next Time _____

Notes _____

_____

_____

_____

_____

Detailed Race Result

Race Name _____ Distance _____ Location _____

Date _____ Time _____ Course Terrain _____

Temperature _____ Weather Conditions _____

Clothes/Shoes/Gear _____

Raced this Event _____ Goals _____

Finish Time _____ Ave. Pace _____ Age _____ Division _____ Age-Grade _____ % = _____

Splits _____

Overall Place _____ / _____ Gender Place _____ / _____ Division Place _____ / _____

Training Plan _____ Gender Winning Time _____ Division Winning Time _____

Special Spectators/Supporters _____

Met _____ Ran With _____

Remember for Next Time _____

Notes _____

_____

_____

_____

_____

Detailed Race Result

Race Name _____ Distance _____ Location _____

Date _____ Time _____ Course Terrain _____

Temperature _____ Weather Conditions _____

Clothes/Shoes/Gear _____

Raced this Event _____ Goals _____

Finish Time _____ Ave. Pace _____ Age _____ Division _____ Age-Grade _____ % = _____

Splits _____

Overall Place _____ / _____ Gender Place _____ / _____ Division Place _____ / _____

Training Plan _____ Gender Winning Time _____ Division Winning Time _____

Special Spectators/Supporters _____

Met _____ Ran With _____

Remember for Next Time _____

Notes _____

_____

_____

_____

_____

Detailed Race Result

Race Name _____ Distance _____ Location _____

Date _____ Time _____ Course Terrain _____

Temperature _____ Weather Conditions _____

Clothes/Shoes/Gear _____

Raced this Event _____ Goals _____

Finish Time _____ Ave. Pace _____ Age _____ Division _____ Age-Grade _____ % = _____

Splits _____

Overall Place _____ / _____ Gender Place _____ / _____ Division Place _____ / _____

Training Plan _____ Gender Winning Time _____ Division Winning Time _____

Special Spectators/Supporters _____

Met _____ Ran With _____

Remember for Next Time _____

Notes _____

_____

_____

_____

_____

Detailed Race Result

Race Name _____ Distance _____ Location _____

Date _____ Time _____ Course Terrain _____

Temperature _____ Weather Conditions _____

Clothes/Shoes/Gear _____

Raced this Event _____ Goals _____

Finish Time _____ Ave. Pace _____ Age _____ Division _____ Age-Grade _____ % = _____

Splits _____

Overall Place _____ / _____ Gender Place _____ / _____ Division Place _____ / _____

Training Plan _____ Gender Winning Time _____ Division Winning Time _____

Special Spectators/Supporters _____

Met _____ Ran With _____

Remember for Next Time _____

Notes _____

_____

_____

_____

_____

Detailed Race Result

Race Name _____ Distance _____ Location _____

Date _____ Time _____ Course Terrain _____

Temperature _____ Weather Conditions _____

Clothes/Shoes/Gear _____

Raced this Event _____ Goals _____

Finish Time _____ Ave. Pace _____ Age _____ Division _____ Age-Grade _____ % = _____

Splits _____

Overall Place _____ / _____ Gender Place _____ / _____ Division Place _____ / _____

Training Plan _____ Gender Winning Time _____ Division Winning Time _____

Special Spectators/Supporters _____

Met _____ Ran With _____

Remember for Next Time _____

Notes _____

_____

_____

_____

_____

_____

Detailed Race Result

Race Name _____ Distance _____ Location _____

Date _____ Time _____ Course Terrain _____

Temperature _____ Weather Conditions _____

Clothes/Shoes/Gear _____

Raced this Event _____ Goals _____

Finish Time _____ Ave. Pace _____ Age _____ Division _____ Age-Grade _____ % = _____

Splits _____

Overall Place _____ / _____ Gender Place _____ / _____ Division Place _____ / _____

Training Plan _____ Gender Winning Time _____ Division Winning Time _____

Special Spectators/Supporters _____

Met _____ Ran With _____

Remember for Next Time _____

Notes _____

_____

_____

_____

_____

Detailed Race Result

Race Name _____ Distance _____ Location _____

Date _____ Time _____ Course Terrain _____

Temperature _____ Weather Conditions _____

Clothes/Shoes/Gear _____

Raced this Event _____ Goals _____

Finish Time _____ Ave. Pace _____ Age _____ Division _____ Age-Grade _____ % = _____

Splits _____

Overall Place _____ / _____ Gender Place _____ / _____ Division Place _____ / _____

Training Plan _____ Gender Winning Time _____ Division Winning Time _____

Special Spectators/Supporters _____

Met _____ Ran With _____

Remember for Next Time _____

Notes _____

_____

_____

_____

_____

Detailed Race Result

Race Name _____ Distance _____ Location _____

Date _____ Time _____ Course Terrain _____

Temperature _____ Weather Conditions _____

Clothes/Shoes/Gear _____

Raced this Event _____ Goals _____

Finish Time _____ Ave. Pace _____ Age _____ Division _____ Age-Grade _____ % = _____

Splits _____

Overall Place _____ / _____ Gender Place _____ / _____ Division Place _____ / _____

Training Plan _____ Gender Winning Time _____ Division Winning Time _____

Special Spectators/Supporters _____

Met _____ Ran With _____

Remember for Next Time _____

Notes _____

_____

_____

_____

_____

_____

Detailed Race Result

Race Name _____ Distance _____ Location _____

Date _____ Time _____ Course Terrain _____

Temperature _____ Weather Conditions _____

Clothes/Shoes/Gear _____

Raced this Event _____ Goals _____

Finish Time _____ Ave. Pace _____ Age _____ Division _____ Age-Grade _____ % = _____

Splits _____

Overall Place _____ / _____ Gender Place _____ / _____ Division Place _____ / _____

Training Plan _____ Gender Winning Time _____ Division Winning Time _____

Special Spectators/Supporters _____

Met _____ Ran With _____

Remember for Next Time _____

Notes _____

_____

_____

_____

_____

_____

Detailed Race Result

Race Name _____ Distance _____ Location _____

Date _____ Time _____ Course Terrain _____

Temperature _____ Weather Conditions _____

Clothes/Shoes/Gear _____

Raced this Event _____ Goals _____

Finish Time _____ Ave. Pace _____ Age _____ Division _____ Age-Grade _____ % = _____

Splits _____

Overall Place _____ / _____ Gender Place _____ / _____ Division Place _____ / _____

Training Plan _____ Gender Winning Time _____ Division Winning Time _____

Special Spectators/Supporters _____

Met _____ Ran With _____

Remember for Next Time _____

Notes _____

_____

_____

_____

_____

Detailed Race Result

Race Name _____ Distance _____ Location _____

Date _____ Time _____ Course Terrain _____

Temperature _____ Weather Conditions _____

Clothes/Shoes/Gear _____

Raced this Event _____ Goals _____

Finish Time _____ Ave. Pace _____ Age _____ Division _____ Age-Grade _____ % = _____

Splits _____

Overall Place _____ / _____ Gender Place _____ / _____ Division Place _____ / _____

Training Plan _____ Gender Winning Time _____ Division Winning Time _____

Special Spectators/Supporters _____

Met _____ Ran With _____

Remember for Next Time _____

Notes _____

_____

_____

_____

_____

Detailed Race Result

Race Name _____ Distance _____ Location _____

Date _____ Time _____ Course Terrain _____

Temperature _____ Weather Conditions _____

Clothes/Shoes/Gear _____

Raced this Event _____ Goals _____

Finish Time _____ Ave. Pace _____ Age _____ Division _____ Age-Grade _____ % = _____

Splits _____

Overall Place _____ / _____ Gender Place _____ / _____ Division Place _____ / _____

Training Plan _____ Gender Winning Time _____ Division Winning Time _____

Special Spectators/Supporters _____

Met _____ Ran With _____

Remember for Next Time _____

Notes _____

_____

_____

_____

_____

Detailed Race Result

Race Name _____ Distance _____ Location _____

Date _____ Time _____ Course Terrain _____

Temperature _____ Weather Conditions _____

Clothes/Shoes/Gear _____

Raced this Event _____ Goals _____

Finish Time _____ Ave. Pace _____ Age _____ Division _____ Age-Grade _____ % =

Splits _____

Overall Place _____ / _____ Gender Place _____ / _____ Division Place _____ / _____

Training Plan _____ Gender Winning Time _____ Division Winning Time _____

Special Spectators/Supporters _____

Met _____ Ran With _____

Remember for Next Time _____

Notes _____

_____

_____

_____

_____

Detailed Race Result

Race Name _____ Distance _____ Location _____

Date _____ Time _____ Course Terrain _____

Temperature _____ Weather Conditions _____

Clothes/Shoes/Gear _____

Raced this Event _____ Goals _____

Finish Time _____ Ave. Pace _____ Age _____ Division _____ Age-Grade _____ % = _____

Splits _____

Overall Place _____ / _____ Gender Place _____ / _____ Division Place _____ / _____

Training Plan _____ Gender Winning Time _____ Division Winning Time _____

Special Spectators/Supporters _____

Met _____ Ran With _____

Remember for Next Time _____

Notes _____

_____

_____

_____

_____

_____

Detailed Race Result

Race Name _____ Distance _____ Location _____

Date _____ Time _____ Course Terrain _____

Temperature _____ Weather Conditions _____

Clothes/Shoes/Gear _____

Raced this Event _____ Goals _____

Finish Time _____ Ave. Pace _____ Age _____ Division _____ Age-Grade _____ % = _____

Splits _____

Overall Place _____ / _____ Gender Place _____ / _____ Division Place _____ / _____

Training Plan _____ Gender Winning Time _____ Division Winning Time _____

Special Spectators/Supporters _____

Met _____ Ran With _____

Remember for Next Time _____

Notes _____

_____

_____

_____

_____

_____

Detailed Race Result

Race Name _____ Distance _____ Location _____

Date _____ Time _____ Course Terrain _____

Temperature _____ Weather Conditions _____

Clothes/Shoes/Gear _____

Raced this Event _____ Goals _____

Finish Time _____ Ave. Pace _____ Age _____ Division _____ Age-Grade _____ % = _____

Splits _____

Overall Place _____ / _____ Gender Place _____ / _____ Division Place _____ / _____

Training Plan _____ Gender Winning Time _____ Division Winning Time _____

Special Spectators/Supporters _____

Met _____ Ran With _____

Remember for Next Time _____

Notes _____

_____

_____

_____

_____

Detailed Race Result

Race Name _____ Distance _____ Location _____

Date _____ Time _____ Course Terrain _____

Temperature _____ Weather Conditions _____

Clothes/Shoes/Gear _____

Raced this Event _____ Goals _____

Finish Time _____ Ave. Pace _____ Age _____ Division _____ Age-Grade _____ % = _____

Splits _____

Overall Place _____ / _____ Gender Place _____ / _____ Division Place _____ / _____

Training Plan _____ Gender Winning Time _____ Division Winning Time _____

Special Spectators/Supporters _____

Met _____ Ran With _____

Remember for Next Time _____

Notes _____

_____

_____

_____

_____

Detailed Race Result

Race Name _____ Distance _____ Location _____

Date _____ Time _____ Course Terrain _____

Temperature _____ Weather Conditions _____

Clothes/Shoes/Gear _____

Raced this Event _____ Goals _____

Finish Time _____ Ave. Pace _____ Age _____ Division _____ Age-Grade _____ % = _____

Splits _____

Overall Place _____ / _____ Gender Place _____ / _____ Division Place _____ / _____

Training Plan _____ Gender Winning Time _____ Division Winning Time _____

Special Spectators/Supporters _____

Met _____ Ran With _____

Remember for Next Time _____

Notes _____

_____

_____

_____

_____

_____

Detailed Race Result

Race Name _____ Distance _____ Location _____

Date _____ Time _____ Course Terrain _____

Temperature _____ Weather Conditions _____

Clothes/Shoes/Gear _____

Raced this Event _____ Goals _____

Finish Time _____ Ave. Pace _____ Age _____ Division _____ Age-Grade _____ % =_____

Splits _____

Overall Place _____ / _____ Gender Place _____ / _____ Division Place _____ / _____

Training Plan _____ Gender Winning Time _____ Division Winning Time _____

Special Spectators/Supporters _____

Met _____ Ran With _____

Remember for Next Time _____

Notes _____

_____

_____

_____

_____

_____

Detailed Race Result

Race Name _____ Distance _____ Location _____

Date _____ Time _____ Course Terrain _____

Temperature _____ Weather Conditions _____

Clothes/Shoes/Gear _____

Raced this Event _____ Goals _____

Finish Time _____ Ave. Pace _____ Age _____ Division _____ Age-Grade _____ % = _____

Splits _____

Overall Place _____ / _____ Gender Place _____ / _____ Division Place _____ / _____

Training Plan _____ Gender Winning Time _____ Division Winning Time _____

Special Spectators/Supporters _____

Met _____ Ran With _____

Remember for Next Time _____

Notes _____

_____

_____

_____

_____

Detailed Race Result

Race Name _____ Distance _____ Location _____

Date _____ Time _____ Course Terrain _____

Temperature _____ Weather Conditions _____

Clothes/Shoes/Gear _____

Raced this Event _____ Goals _____

Finish Time _____ Ave. Pace _____ Age _____ Division _____ Age-Grade _____ % = _____

Splits _____

Overall Place _____ / _____ Gender Place _____ / _____ Division Place _____ / _____

Training Plan _____ Gender Winning Time _____ Division Winning Time _____

Special Spectators/Supporters _____

Met _____ Ran With _____

Remember for Next Time _____

Notes _____

_____

_____

_____

_____

_____

Detailed Race Result

Race Name _____ Distance _____ Location _____

Date _____ Time _____ Course Terrain _____

Temperature _____ Weather Conditions _____

Clothes/Shoes/Gear _____

Raced this Event _____ Goals _____

Finish Time _____ Ave. Pace _____ Age _____ Division _____ Age-Grade _____ % = _____

Splits _____

Overall Place _____/_____ Gender Place _____/_____ Division Place _____/_____

Training Plan _____ Gender Winning Time _____ Division Winning Time _____

Special Spectators/Supporters _____

Met _____ Ran With _____

Remember for Next Time _____

Notes _____

_____

_____

_____

_____

Detailed Race Result

Race Name _____ Distance _____ Location _____

Date _____ Time _____ Course Terrain _____

Temperature _____ Weather Conditions _____

Clothes/Shoes/Gear _____

Raced this Event _____ Goals _____

Finish Time _____ Ave. Pace _____ Age _____ Division _____ Age-Grade _____ % = _____

Splits _____

Overall Place _____ / _____ Gender Place _____ / _____ Division Place _____ / _____

Training Plan _____ Gender Winning Time _____ Division Winning Time _____

Special Spectators/Supporters _____

Met _____ Ran With _____

Remember for Next Time _____

Notes _____

_____

_____

_____

_____

Detailed Race Result

Race Name _____ Distance _____ Location _____

Date _____ Time _____ Course Terrain _____

Temperature _____ Weather Conditions _____

Clothes/Shoes/Gear _____

Raced this Event _____ Goals _____

Finish Time _____ Ave. Pace _____ Age _____ Division _____ Age-Grade _____ % = _____

Splits _____

Overall Place _____ / _____ Gender Place _____ / _____ Division Place _____ / _____

Training Plan _____ Gender Winning Time _____ Division Winning Time _____

Special Spectators/Supporters _____

Met _____ Ran With _____

Remember for Next Time _____

Notes _____

_____

_____

_____

_____

Detailed Race Result

Race Name _____ Distance _____ Location _____

Date _____ Time _____ Course Terrain _____

Temperature _____ Weather Conditions _____

Clothes/Shoes/Gear _____

Raced this Event _____ Goals _____

Finish Time _____ Ave. Pace _____ Age _____ Division _____ Age-Grade _____ % = _____

Splits_____

Overall Place _____ / _____ Gender Place _____ / _____ Division Place _____ / _____

Training Plan _____ Gender Winning Time _____ Division Winning Time _____

Special Spectators/Supporters _____

Met _____ Ran With _____

Remember for Next Time _____

Notes _____

_____

_____

_____

_____

Detailed Race Result

Race Name _____ Distance _____ Location _____

Date _____ Time _____ Course Terrain _____

Temperature _____ Weather Conditions _____

Clothes/Shoes/Gear _____

Raced this Event _____ Goals _____

Finish Time _____ Ave. Pace _____ Age _____ Division _____ Age-Grade _____ % = _____

Splits _____

Overall Place _____ / _____ Gender Place _____ / _____ Division Place _____ / _____

Training Plan _____ Gender Winning Time _____ Division Winning Time _____

Special Spectators/Supporters _____

Met _____ Ran With _____

Remember for Next Time _____

Notes _____

_____

_____

_____

_____

Detailed Race Result

Race Name _____ Distance _____ Location _____

Date _____ Time _____ Course Terrain _____

Temperature _____ Weather Conditions _____

Clothes/Shoes/Gear _____

Raced this Event _____ Goals _____

Finish Time _____ Ave. Pace _____ Age _____ Division _____ Age-Grade _____ % = _____

Splits _____

Overall Place _____ / _____ Gender Place _____ / _____ Division Place _____ / _____

Training Plan _____ Gender Winning Time _____ Division Winning Time _____

Special Spectators/Supporters _____

Met _____ Ran With _____

Remember for Next Time _____

Notes _____

_____

_____

_____

_____

Detailed Race Result

Race Name _____ Distance _____ Location _____

Date _____ Time _____ Course Terrain _____

Temperature _____ Weather Conditions _____

Clothes/Shoes/Gear _____

Raced this Event _____ Goals _____

Finish Time _____ Ave. Pace _____ Age _____ Division _____ Age-Grade _____ % = _____

Splits _____

Overall Place _____/_____ Gender Place _____/_____ Division Place _____/_____

Training Plan _____ Gender Winning Time _____ Division Winning Time _____

Special Spectators/Supporters _____

Met _____ Ran With _____

Remember for Next Time _____

Notes _____

_____

_____

_____

_____

Detailed Race Result

Race Name _____ Distance _____ Location _____

Date _____ Time _____ Course Terrain _____

Temperature _____ Weather Conditions _____

Clothes/Shoes/Gear _____

Raced this Event _____ Goals _____

Finish Time _____ Ave. Pace _____ Age _____ Division _____ Age-Grade _____ % = _____

Splits _____

Overall Place _____ / _____ Gender Place _____ / _____ Division Place _____ / _____

Training Plan _____ Gender Winning Time _____ Division Winning Time _____

Special Spectators/Supporters _____

Met _____ Ran With _____

Remember for Next Time _____

Notes _____

_____

_____

_____

_____

_____

Detailed Race Result

Race Name _____ Distance _____ Location _____

Date _____ Time _____ Course Terrain _____

Temperature _____ Weather Conditions _____

Clothes/Shoes/Gear _____

Raced this Event _____ Goals _____

Finish Time _____ Ave. Pace _____ Age _____ Division _____ Age-Grade _____ % = _____

Splits _____

Overall Place _____ / _____ Gender Place _____ / _____ Division Place _____ / _____

Training Plan _____ Gender Winning Time _____ Division Winning Time _____

Special Spectators/Supporters _____

Met _____ Ran With _____

Remember for Next Time _____

Notes _____

_____

_____

_____

_____

Detailed Race Result

Race Name _____ Distance _____ Location _____

Date _____ Time _____ Course Terrain _____

Temperature _____ Weather Conditions _____

Clothes/Shoes/Gear _____

Raced this Event _____ Goals _____

Finish Time _____ Ave. Pace _____ Age _____ Division _____ Age-Grade _____ % = _____

Splits _____

Overall Place _____ / _____ Gender Place _____ / _____ Division Place _____ / _____

Training Plan _____ Gender Winning Time _____ Division Winning Time _____

Special Spectators/Supporters _____

Met _____ Ran With _____

Remember for Next Time _____

Notes _____

_____

_____

_____

_____

Detailed Race Result

Race Name _____ Distance _____ Location _____

Date _____ Time _____ Course Terrain _____

Temperature _____ Weather Conditions _____

Clothes/Shoes/Gear _____

Raced this Event _____ Goals _____

Finish Time _____ Ave. Pace _____ Age _____ Division _____ Age-Grade _____ % = _____

Splits _____

Overall Place _____ / _____ Gender Place _____ / _____ Division Place _____ / _____

Training Plan _____ Gender Winning Time _____ Division Winning Time _____

Special Spectators/Supporters _____

Met _____ Ran With _____

Remember for Next Time _____

Notes _____

_____

_____

_____

_____

Detailed Race Result

Race Name _____ Distance _____ Location _____

Date _____ Time _____ Course Terrain _____

Temperature _____ Weather Conditions _____

Clothes/Shoes/Gear _____

Raced this Event _____ Goals _____

Finish Time _____ Ave. Pace _____ Age _____ Division _____ Age-Grade _____ % = _____

Splits _____

Overall Place _____ / _____ Gender Place _____ / _____ Division Place _____ / _____

Training Plan _____ Gender Winning Time _____ Division Winning Time _____

Special Spectators/Supporters _____

Met _____ Ran With _____

Remember for Next Time _____

Notes _____

_____

_____

_____

_____

Detailed Race Result

Race Name _____ Distance _____ Location _____

Date _____ Time _____ Course Terrain _____

Temperature _____ Weather Conditions _____

Clothes/Shoes/Gear _____

Raced this Event _____ Goals _____

Finish Time _____ Ave. Pace _____ Age _____ Division _____ Age-Grade _____ % = _____

Splits _____

Overall Place _____ / _____ Gender Place _____ / _____ Division Place _____ / _____

Training Plan _____ Gender Winning Time _____ Division Winning Time _____

Special Spectators/Supporters _____

Met _____ Ran With _____

Remember for Next Time _____

Notes _____

_____

_____

_____

_____

Detailed Race Result

Race Name _____ Distance _____ Location _____

Date _____ Time _____ Course Terrain _____

Temperature _____ Weather Conditions _____

Clothes/Shoes/Gear _____

Raced this Event _____ Goals _____

Finish Time _____ Ave. Pace _____ Age _____ Division _____ Age-Grade _____ % = _____

Splits _____

Overall Place _____ / _____ Gender Place _____ / _____ Division Place _____ / _____

Training Plan _____ Gender Winning Time _____ Division Winning Time _____

Special Spectators/Supporters _____

Met _____ Ran With _____

Remember for Next Time _____

Notes _____

_____

_____

_____

_____

Detailed Race Result

Race Name _____ Distance _____ Location _____

Date _____ Time _____ Course Terrain _____

Temperature _____ Weather Conditions _____

Clothes/Shoes/Gear _____

Raced this Event _____ Goals _____

Finish Time _____ Ave. Pace _____ Age _____ Division _____ Age-Grade _____ % = _____

Splits _____

Overall Place _____ / _____ Gender Place _____ / _____ Division Place _____ / _____

Training Plan _____ Gender Winning Time _____ Division Winning Time _____

Special Spectators/Supporters _____

Met _____ Ran With _____

Remember for Next Time _____

Notes _____

_____

_____

_____

_____

_____

Detailed Race Result

Race Name _____ Distance _____ Location _____

Date _____ Time _____ Course Terrain _____

Temperature _____ Weather Conditions _____

Clothes/Shoes/Gear _____

Raced this Event _____ Goals _____

Finish Time _____ Ave. Pace _____ Age _____ Division _____ Age-Grade _____ % = _____

Splits _____

Overall Place _____ / _____ Gender Place _____ / _____ Division Place _____ / _____

Training Plan _____ Gender Winning Time _____ Division Winning Time _____

Special Spectators/Supporters _____

Met _____ Ran With _____

Remember for Next Time _____

Notes _____

_____

_____

_____

_____

_____

Detailed Race Result

Race Name _____ Distance _____ Location _____

Date _____ Time _____ Course Terrain _____

Temperature _____ Weather Conditions _____

Clothes/Shoes/Gear _____

Raced this Event _____ Goals _____

Finish Time _____ Ave. Pace _____ Age _____ Division _____ Age-Grade _____ % = _____

Splits _____

Overall Place _____ / _____ Gender Place _____ / _____ Division Place _____ / _____

Training Plan _____ Gender Winning Time _____ Division Winning Time _____

Special Spectators/Supporters _____

Met _____ Ran With _____

Remember for Next Time _____

Notes _____

_____

_____

_____

_____

Detailed Race Result

Race Name _____ Distance _____ Location _____

Date _____ Time _____ Course Terrain _____

Temperature _____ Weather Conditions _____

Clothes/Shoes/Gear _____

Raced this Event _____ Goals _____

Finish Time _____ Ave. Pace _____ Age _____ Division _____ Age-Grade _____ % = _____

Splits _____

Overall Place _____ / _____ Gender Place _____ / _____ Division Place _____ / _____

Training Plan _____ Gender Winning Time _____ Division Winning Time _____

Special Spectators/Supporters _____

Met _____ Ran With _____

Remember for Next Time _____

Notes _____

_____

_____

_____

_____

Detailed Race Result

Race Name _____ Distance _____ Location _____

Date _____ Time _____ Course Terrain _____

Temperature _____ Weather Conditions _____

Clothes/Shoes/Gear _____

Raced this Event _____ Goals _____

Finish Time _____ Ave. Pace _____ Age _____ Division _____ Age-Grade _____ % = _____

Splits _____

Overall Place _____ / _____ Gender Place _____ / _____ Division Place _____ / _____

Training Plan _____ Gender Winning Time _____ Division Winning Time _____

Special Spectators/Supporters _____

Met _____ Ran With _____

Remember for Next Time _____

Notes _____

_____

_____

_____

_____

Detailed Race Result

Race Name _____ Distance _____ Location _____

Date _____ Time _____ Course Terrain _____

Temperature _____ Weather Conditions _____

Clothes/Shoes/Gear _____

Raced this Event _____ Goals _____

Finish Time _____ Ave. Pace _____ Age _____ Division _____ Age-Grade _____ % = _____

Splits _____

Overall Place _____/_____ Gender Place _____/_____ Division Place _____/_____

Training Plan _____ Gender Winning Time _____ Division Winning Time _____

Special Spectators/Supporters _____

Met _____ Ran With _____

Remember for Next Time _____

Notes _____

_____

_____

_____

_____

Detailed Race Result

Race Name _____ Distance _____ Location _____

Date _____ Time _____ Course Terrain _____

Temperature _____ Weather Conditions _____

Clothes/Shoes/Gear _____

Raced this Event _____ Goals _____

Finish Time _____ Ave. Pace _____ Age _____ Division _____ Age-Grade _____ % = _____

Splits _____

Overall Place _____ / _____ Gender Place _____ / _____ Division Place _____ / _____

Training Plan _____ Gender Winning Time _____ Division Winning Time _____

Special Spectators/Supporters _____

Met _____ Ran With _____

Remember for Next Time _____

Notes _____

_____

_____

_____

_____

Detailed Race Result

Race Name _____ Distance _____ Location _____

Date _____ Time _____ Course Terrain _____

Temperature _____ Weather Conditions _____

Clothes/Shoes/Gear _____

Raced this Event _____ Goals _____

Finish Time _____ Ave. Pace _____ Age _____ Division _____ Age-Grade _____ % = _____

Splits _____

Overall Place _____ / _____ Gender Place _____ / _____ Division Place _____ / _____

Training Plan _____ Gender Winning Time _____ Division Winning Time _____

Special Spectators/Supporters _____

Met _____ Ran With _____

Remember for Next Time _____

Notes _____

_____

_____

_____

_____

Detailed Race Result

Race Name _____ Distance _____ Location _____

Date _____ Time _____ Course Terrain _____

Temperature _____ Weather Conditions _____

Clothes/Shoes/Gear _____

Raced this Event _____ Goals _____

Finish Time _____ Ave. Pace _____ Age _____ Division _____ Age-Grade _____ % = _____

Splits _____

Overall Place _____ / _____ Gender Place _____ / _____ Division Place _____ / _____

Training Plan _____ Gender Winning Time _____ Division Winning Time _____

Special Spectators/Supporters _____

Met _____ Ran With _____

Remember for Next Time _____

Notes _____

_____

_____

_____

_____

Detailed Race Result

Race Name _____ Distance _____ Location _____

Date _____ Time _____ Course Terrain _____

Temperature _____ Weather Conditions _____

Clothes/Shoes/Gear _____

Raced this Event _____ Goals _____

Finish Time _____ Ave. Pace _____ Age _____ Division _____ Age-Grade _____ % = _____

Splits _____

Overall Place _____ / _____ Gender Place _____ / _____ Division Place _____ / _____

Training Plan _____ Gender Winning Time _____ Division Winning Time _____

Special Spectators/Supporters _____

Met _____ Ran With _____

Remember for Next Time _____

Notes _____

_____

_____

_____

_____

Detailed Race Result

Race Name _____ Distance _____ Location _____

Date _____ Time _____ Course Terrain _____

Temperature _____ Weather Conditions _____

Clothes/Shoes/Gear _____

Raced this Event _____ Goals _____

Finish Time _____ Ave. Pace _____ Age _____ Division _____ Age-Grade _____ % = _____

Splits _____

Overall Place _____ / _____ Gender Place _____ / _____ Division Place _____ / _____

Training Plan _____ Gender Winning Time _____ Division Winning Time _____

Special Spectators/Supporters _____

Met _____ Ran With _____

Remember for Next Time _____

Notes _____

_____

_____

_____

_____

Detailed Race Result

Race Name _____ Distance _____ Location _____

Date _____ Time _____ Course Terrain _____

Temperature _____ Weather Conditions _____

Clothes/Shoes/Gear _____

Raced this Event _____ Goals _____

Finish Time _____ Ave. Pace _____ Age _____ Division _____ Age-Grade _____ % = _____

Splits_____

Overall Place _____ / _____ Gender Place _____ / _____ Division Place _____ / _____

Training Plan _____ Gender Winning Time _____ Division Winning Time _____

Special Spectators/Supporters _____

Met _____ Ran With _____

Remember for Next Time _____

Notes _____

_____

_____

_____

_____

_____

Detailed Race Result

Race Name _____ Distance _____ Location _____

Date _____ Time _____ Course Terrain _____

Temperature _____ Weather Conditions _____

Clothes/Shoes/Gear _____

Raced this Event _____ Goals _____

Finish Time _____ Ave. Pace _____ Age ____ Division _____ Age-Grade _____ % = _____

Splits _____

Overall Place _____ / _____ Gender Place _____ / _____ Division Place _____ / _____

Training Plan _____ Gender Winning Time _____ Division Winning Time _____

Special Spectators/Supporters _____

Met _____ Ran With _____

Remember for Next Time _____

Notes _____

_____

_____

_____

_____

Repeat Race Results

Race Name _____ Distance _____ Location _____

Date	Time	Finish Time	Pace	Overall Place	Gender Place	Division Place	Ref. Pg.

Notes_____

_____

_____

Repeat Race Results

Race Name _____ Distance _____ Location _____

Date	Time	Finish Time	Pace	Overall Place	Gender Place	Division Place	Ref. Pg.

Notes _____

_____

_____

Repeat Race Results

Race Name _____ Distance _____ Location _____

Date	Time	Finish Time	Pace	Overall Place	Gender Place	Division Place	Ref. Pg.

Notes _____

_____

_____

Repeat Race Results

Race Name _____ Distance _____ Location _____

Date	Time	Finish Time	Pace	Overall Place	Gender Place	Division Place	Ref. Pg.

Notes _____

_____

_____

Repeat Race Results

Race Name _____ Distance _____ Location _____

Date	Time	Finish Time	Pace	Overall Place	Gender Place	Division Place	Ref. Pg.

Notes _____

_____

_____

Repeat Race Results

Race Name _____ Distance _____ Location _____

Date	Time	Finish Time	Pace	Overall Place	Gender Place	Division Place	Ref. Pg.

Notes _____

_____

_____

Repeat Race Results

Race Name _____ Distance _____ Location _____

Date	Time	Finish Time	Pace	Overall Place	Gender Place	Division Place	Ref. Pg.

Notes _____

_____

_____

Repeat Race Results

Race Name _____ Distance _____ Location _____

Date	Time	Finish Time	Pace	Overall Place	Gender Place	Division Place	Ref. Pg.

Notes _____

_____

_____

Repeat Race Results

Race Name _____ Distance _____ Location _____

Date	Time	Finish Time	Pace	Overall Place	Gender Place	Division Place	Ref. Pg.

Notes _____

_____

_____

Repeat Race Results

Race Name _____ Distance _____ Location _____

Date	Time	Finish Time	Pace	Overall Place	Gender Place	Division Place	Ref. Pg.

Notes_____

_____

_____

Repeat Race Results

Race Name _____ Distance _____ Location _____

Date	Time	Finish Time	Pace	Overall Place	Gender Place	Division Place	Ref. Pg.

Notes _____

_____

_____

Top Race Performances—Top 5 PR's by Distance (*suggestion—write in pencil for future faster times)

Race Distance _____

Date	Age	Race Name	Location	Finish Time	Pace	Place	Ref. Pg.

Race Distance _____

Date	Age	Race Name	Location	Finish Time	Pace	Place	Ref. Pg.

Top Race Performances—Top 5 PR's by Distance (*suggestion—write in pencil for future faster times)

Race Distance _____

Date	Age	Race Name	Location	Finish Time	Pace	Place	Ref. Pg.

Race Distance _____

Date	Age	Race Name	Location	Finish Time	Pace	Place	Ref. Pg.

Top Race Performances—Top 5 PR's by Distance (*suggestion—write in pencil for future faster times)

Race Distance _____

Date	Age	Race Name	Location	Finish Time	Pace	Place	Ref. Pg.

Race Distance _____

Date	Age	Race Name	Location	Finish Time	Pace	Place	Ref. Pg.

Top Race Performances—Top 5 PR's by Distance (*suggestion—write in pencil for future faster times)

Race Distance _____

Date	Age	Race Name	Location	Finish Time	Pace	Place	Ref. Pg.

Race Distance _____

Date	Age	Race Name	Location	Finish Time	Pace	Place	Ref. Pg.

Top Race Performances—Top 5 PR's by Distance (*suggestion—write in pencil for future faster times)

Race Distance _____

Date	Age	Race Name	Location	Finish Time	Pace	Place	Ref. Pg.

Race Distance _____

Date	Age	Race Name	Location	Finish Time	Pace	Place	Ref. Pg.

Top Race Performances—Top 5 PR's by Distance (*suggestion—write in pencil for future faster times)

Race Distance _____

Date	Age	Race Name	Location	Finish Time	Pace	Place	Ref. Pg.

Race Distance _____

Date	Age	Race Name	Location	Finish Time	Pace	Place	Ref. Pg.

Master Runner (40+) Top Race Performances—PR by Distance

Race Distance_____ Finish Time_____ Age-Grade Adjusted Time_____ %_____

Date	Age	Race Name	Location	Pace	Place	Ref. Pg.

Race Distance_____ Finish Time_____ Age-Grade Adjusted Time_____ %_____

Date	Age	Race Name	Location	Pace	Place	Ref. Pg.

Race Distance_____ Finish Time_____ Age-Grade Adjusted Time_____ %_____

Date	Age	Race Name	Location	Pace	Place	Ref. Pg.

Race Distance_____ Finish Time_____ Age-Grade Adjusted Time_____ %_____

Date	Age	Race Name	Location	Pace	Place	Ref. Pg.

Master Runner (40+) Top Race Performances—PR by Distance

Race Distance_____ Finish Time_____ Age-Grade Adjusted Time_____ %_____

Date	Age	Race Name	Location	Pace	Place	Ref. Pg.

Race Distance_____ Finish Time_____ Age-Grade Adjusted Time_____ %_____

Date	Age	Race Name	Location	Pace	Place	Ref. Pg.

Race Distance_____ Finish Time_____ Age-Grade Adjusted Time_____ %_____

Date	Age	Race Name	Location	Pace	Place	Ref. Pg.

Race Distance_____ Finish Time_____ Age-Grade Adjusted Time_____ %_____

Date	Age	Race Name	Location	Pace	Place	Ref. Pg.

Grand Master Runner (50+) Top Race Performances—PR by Distance

Race Distance_____ Finish Time_____ Age-Grade Adjusted Time_____ %_____

Date	Age	Race Name	Location	Pace	Place	Ref. Pg.

Race Distance_____ Finish Time_____ Age-Grade Adjusted Time_____ %_____

Date	Age	Race Name	Location	Pace	Place	Ref. Pg.

Race Distance_____ Finish Time_____ Age-Grade Adjusted Time_____ %_____

Date	Age	Race Name	Location	Pace	Place	Ref. Pg.

Race Distance_____ Finish Time_____ Age-Grade Adjusted Time_____ %_____

Date	Age	Race Name	Location	Pace	Place	Ref. Pg.

Grand Master Runner (50+) Top Race Performances—PR by Distance

Race Distance_____ Finish Time_____ Age-Grade Adjusted Time_____ %_____

Date	Age	Race Name	Location	Pace	Place	Ref. Pg.

Race Distance_____ Finish Time_____ Age-Grade Adjusted Time_____ %_____

Date	Age	Race Name	Location	Pace	Place	Ref. Pg.

Race Distance_____ Finish Time_____ Age-Grade Adjusted Time_____ %_____

Date	Age	Race Name	Location	Pace	Place	Ref. Pg.

Race Distance_____ Finish Time_____ Age-Grade Adjusted Time_____ %_____

Date	Age	Race Name	Location	Pace	Place	Ref. Pg.

Senior Grand Master Runner (60+) Top Race Performances—PR by Distance

Race Distance_____ Finish Time_____ Age-Grade Adjusted Time_____ %_____

Date	Age	Race Name	Location	Pace	Place	Ref. Pg.

Race Distance_____ Finish Time_____ Age-Grade Adjusted Time_____ %_____

Date	Age	Race Name	Location	Pace	Place	Ref. Pg.

Race Distance_____ Finish Time_____ Age-Grade Adjusted Time_____ %_____

Date	Age	Race Name	Location	Pace	Place	Ref. Pg.

Race Distance_____ Finish Time_____ Age-Grade Adjusted Time_____ %_____

Date	Age	Race Name	Location	Pace	Place	Ref. Pg.

Senior Grand Master Runner (60+) Top Race Performances—PR by Distance

Race Distance_____ Finish Time_____ Age-Grade Adjusted Time_____ %_____

Date	Age	Race Name	Location	Pace	Place	Ref. Pg.

Race Distance_____ Finish Time_____ Age-Grade Adjusted Time_____ %_____

Date	Age	Race Name	Location	Pace	Place	Ref. Pg.

Race Distance_____ Finish Time_____ Age-Grade Adjusted Time_____ %_____

Date	Age	Race Name	Location	Pace	Place	Ref. Pg.

Race Distance_____ Finish Time_____ Age-Grade Adjusted Time_____ %_____

Date	Age	Race Name	Location	Pace	Place	Ref. Pg.

Results by Race Distance—_____

Date	Race Name	Location	Finish Time	Pace	Place	Ref. Pg.

Results by Race Distance—_____

Date	Race Name	Location	Finish Time	Pace	Place	Ref. Pg.

Results by Race Distance—_____

Date	Race Name	Location	Finish Time	Pace	Place	Ref. Pg.

Results by Race Distance—_____

Date	Race Name	Location	Finish Time	Pace	Place	Ref. Pg.

Results by Race Distance— _____

Date	Race Name	Location	Finish Time	Pace	Place	Ref. Pg.

Results by Race Distance—_____

Date	Race Name	Location	Finish Time	Pace	Place	Ref. Pg.

Results by Race Distance—_____

Date	Race Name	Location	Finish Time	Pace	Place	Ref. Pg.

Results by Race Distance— _____

Date	Race Name	Location	Finish Time	Pace	Place	Ref. Pg.

Results by Race Distance—_____

Date	Race Name	Location	Finish Time	Pace	Place	Ref. Pg.

Results by Race Distance—_____

Date	Race Name	Location	Finish Time	Pace	Place	Ref. Pg.

Results by Race Distance— _____

Date	Race Name	Location	Finish Time	Pace	Place	Ref. Pg.

Results by Race Distance—_____

Date	Race Name	Location	Finish Time	Pace	Place	Ref. Pg.

United States of America

Quick Reference Map—
Mark your **Destination Races**

Run the Country—Destination Races

Date	Location	Race Name	Distance	Finish Time	Ref. Pg.

Finish Line Achievements—The Runner's Ultimate Racing Journal

Run the Country—Destination Races

Date	Location	Race Name	Distance	Finish Time	Ref. Pg.

Run the Country—Destination Races

Date	Location	Race Name	Distance	Finish Time	Ref. Pg.

United States of America

Quick Reference Map—
Mark your completed states for
50 States Marathon Quest

50 States Marathon Quest

	Date	State	Race Name	Location	Finish Time	Ref. Pg.
1						
2						
3						
4						
5						
6						
7						
8						
9						
10						
11						
12						
13						
14						
15						
16						
17						

Finish Line Achievements—The Runner's Ultimate Racing Journal

50 States Marathon Quest

	Date	State	Race Name	Location	Finish Time	Ref. Pg.
18						
19						
20						
21						
22						
23						
24						
25						
26						
27						
28						
29						
30						
31						
32						
33						
34						

50 States Marathon Quest

	Date	State	Race Name	Location	Finish Time	Ref. Pg.
35						
36						
37						
38						
39						
40						
41						
42						
43						
44						
45						
46						
47						
48						
49						
50						

50 States Plus D.C. Marathon Quest

	Date	State	Race Name	Location	Finish Time	Ref. Pg.
51						

Membership with a 50 State Club? _____

Favorite 50 State Marathon _____

Most Challenging 50 State Marathon _____

Notes _____

_____

_____

_____

_____

_____

_____

_____

_____

United States of America

Quick Reference Map—
Mark your completed states for
50 States Half Marathon Goal

50 States Half Marathon Goal

	Date	State	Race Name	Location	Finish Time	Ref. Pg.
1						
2						
3						
4						
5						
6						
7						
8						
9						
10						
11						
12						
13						
14						
15						
16						
17						

50 States Half Marathon Goal

	Date	State	Race Name	Location	Finish Time	Ref. Pg.
18						
19						
20						
21						
22						
23						
24						
25						
26						
27						
28						
29						
30						
31						
32						
33						
34						

50 States Half Marathon Goal

	Date	State	Race Name	Location	Finish Time	Ref. Pg.
35						
36						
37						
38						
39						
40						
41						
42						
43						
44						
45						
46						
47						
48						
49						
50						

Membership with a 50 State Club? _____

Favorite 50 State Half Marathon _____

Most Challenging 50 State Half Marathon _____

Notes _____

_____

_____

_____

_____

_____

_____

_____

_____

_____

_____

_____

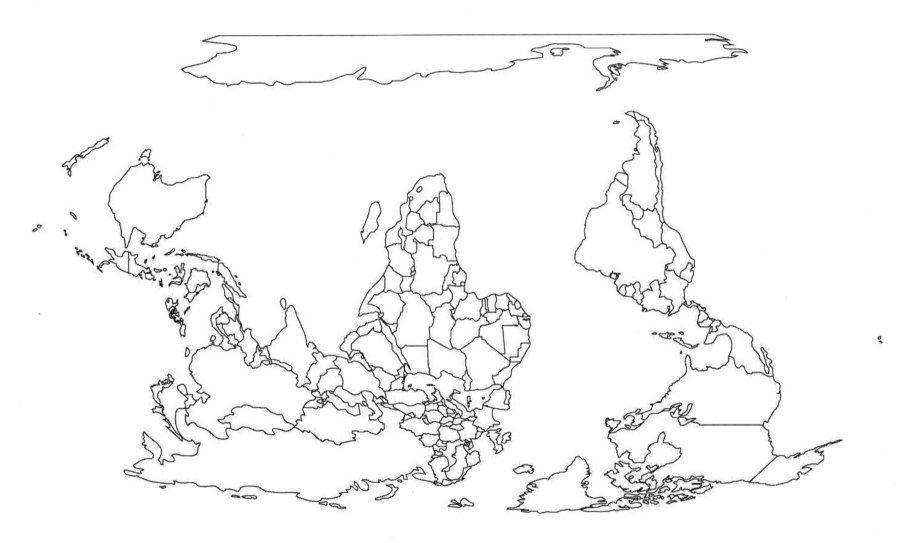

Quick Reference Map—Mark your completed International Destination Races

Run the World—International Destination Races

Date	Country	Race Name	Location	Distance	Finish Time	Ref. Pg.

7 Continents Expedition—Race Distance_____

	Date	Continent	Race Name	Location / Country	Finish Time	Ref. Pg.
1						
2						
3						
4						
5						
6						
7						

Continents – Please consult specific continents at www.worldatlas.com for area breakdown of each.

North America

South America

Europe

Asia

Africa

Oceana

Antarctica

Notes_____

Other Adventurous Endeavors

Date	Location	Race Name	Type/Distance	Finish Time	Ref. Pg.

Other Adventurous Endeavors

Date	Location	Race Name	Type/Distance	Finish Time	Ref. Pg.

Future Race Goal Checklist

_____
_____
_____
_____
_____
_____
_____
_____
_____
_____
_____
_____
_____
_____
_____
_____

Races-To-Do Bucket List

_____
_____
_____
_____
_____
_____
_____
_____
_____
_____
_____
_____
_____
_____
_____

Charitable Funds Raised/Donated

Date	Race Name	Location	$ Raised/Donated	For	Sub-Total

Total $ _____

Charitable Funds Raised/Donated

Date	Race Name	Location	$ Raised/Donated	For	Sub-Total

Total $ _____

Notes

Mile Pace Chart

1 MILE	5K (3.1M)	5 MILE	10K (6.2M)	15K (9.3M)	10 MILE	13.1 MILE	15 MILE	30K (18.64M)	20 MILE	25 MILE	26.2	
5:00	15:32	25:00	31:04	46:36	50:00	1:05:33	1:15:00	1:33:12	1:40:00	2:05:00	2:11:05	
5:20	16:34	26:40	33:08	49:42	53:20	1:09:55	1:20:00	1:39:24	1:46:40	2:13:20	2:19:49	
5:40	17:36	28:20	35:12	52:48	56:40	1:14:17	1:25:00	1:45:36	1:53:20	2:21:40	2:28:33	
6:00	18:38	30:00	37:17	55:54	1:00:00	1:18:39	1:30:00	1:51:48	2:00:00	2:30:00	2:37:17	
6:20	19:40	31:40	39:22	59:00	1:03:20	1:23:01	1:35:00	1:58:00	2:08:40	2:38:20	2:46:01	
6:40	20:42	33:20	41:26	1:02:06	1:06:40	1:27:23	1:40:00	2:04:12	2:13:20	2:46:40	2:54:45	
7:00	21:44	35:00	43:30	1:05:12	1:10:00	1:31:45	1:45:00	2:10:24	2:20:00	2:55:00	3:03:29	
7:20	22:46	36:40	45:34	1:08:18	1:13:20	1:36:07	1:50:00	2:16:36	2:26:40	3:03:20	3:12:13	
7:40	23:48	38:20	47:38	1:11:24	1:16:40	1:40:29	1:55:00	2:22:48	2:33:20	3:11:40	3:20:57	
8:00	24:50	40:00	49:42	1:14:30	1:20:00	1:44:51	2:00:00	2:29:00	2:40:00	3:20:00	3:29:41	
8:20	25:52	41:40	51:46	1:17:36	1:23:20	1:49:13	2:05:00	2:35:12	2:46:40	3:28:20	3:38:25	
8:40	26:54	43:20	53:50	1:20:42	1:26:40	1:53:35	2:10:00	2:41:24	2:53:20	3:36:40	3:47:09	
9:00	27:56	45:00	55:54	1:23:48	1:30:00	1:57:57	2:15:00	2:47:36	3:00:00	3:45:00	3:55:53	
9:20	28:58	46:40	57:58	1:26:54	1:33:20	2:02:19	2:20:00	2:53:48	3:06:40	3:53:20	4:04:37	
9:40	30:00	48:20	1:00:02	1:30:00	1:36:40	2:06:41	2:25:00	3:00:00	3:13:20	4:01:40	4:13:21	
10:00	31:02	50:00	1:02:06	1:33:06	1:40:00	2:11:03	2:30:00	3:06:12	3:20:00	4:10:00	4:22:05	
10:20	32:04	51:40	1:04:10	1:36:12	1:43:20	2:15:25	2:35:00	3:12:24	3:28:40	4:18:20	4:30:49	
10:40	33:06	53:20	1:06:14	1:39:18	1:46:40	2:19:47	2:40:00	3:18:36	3:33:20	4:26:40	4:39:33	
11:00	34:08	55:00	1:08:18	1:42:24	1:50:00	2:24:09	2:45:00	3:24:48	3:40:00	4:35:00	4:48:17	
11:20	35:10	56:40	1:10:22	1:45:30	1:53:20	2:28:31	2:50:00	3:31:00	3:46:40	4:43:20	4:57:01	
11:40	36:12	58:20	1:12:26	1:48:36	1:56:40	2:32:53	2:55:00	3:37:12	3:53:20	4:51:40	5:05:45	
12:00	37:14	1:00:00	1:14:30	1:51:42	2:00:00	2:37:15	3:00:00	3:43:24	4:00:00	5:00:00	5:14:29	
12:30	38:47	1:02:30	1:17:36	1:56:21	2:05:00	2:43:48	3:07:30	3:51:42	4:10:00	5:12:30	5:27:35	
13:00	40:20	1:05:00	1:20:42	2:01:00	2:10:00	2:50:21	3:15:00	4:00:00	4:20:00	5:25:00	5:40:41	
13:30	41:53	1:07:30	1:23:48	2:05:39	2:15:50	2:56:54	3:22:30	4:11:18	4:30:00	5:37:30	5:53:47	
14:00	43:26	1:10:00	1:26:54	2:10:18	2:20:00	3:03:27	3:30:00	4:20:36	4:40:00	5:50:00	6:06:53	

Kilometer Pace Chart

1KM	3K	5K	10K	15K	20K	21.1K (13.1M)	25K	30K	35K	40K	42.2K (26.2M)	
3:00	9:00	15:00	30:00	45:00	1:00:00	1:03:18	1:15:00	1:30:00	1:45:00	2:00:00	2:06:36	
3:15	9:45	16:15	32:30	48:45	1:05:00	1:08:35	1:21:15	1:37:30	1:53:45	2:10:00	2:16:30	
3:30	10:30	17:30	35:10	52:30	1:10:00	1:13:51	1:27:30	1:45:00	2:02:30	2:20:00	2:27:42	
3:45	11:15	18:45	37:30	56:15	1:15:00	1:19:08	1:33:45	1:52:30	2:11:15	2:30:00	2:38:15	
4:00	12:00	20:00	40:00	1:00:00	1:20:00	1:24:24	1:40:00	2:00:00	2:20:00	2:40:00	2:48:48	
4:15	12:45	21:15	42:30	1:03:45	1:25:00	1:29:40	1:46:15	2:07:30	2:28:45	2:50:00	2:59:21	
4:30	13:30	22:30	45:00	1:07:30	1:30:00	1:34:57	1:52:30	2:15:00	2:37:30	3:00:00	3:09:54	
4:45	14:15	23:45	47:30	1:11:15	1:35:00	1:40:13	1:58:45	2:22:30	2:46:15	3:10:00	3:20:27	
5:00	15:00	25:00	50:00	1:15:00	1:40:00	1:45:30	2:05:00	2:30:00	2:55:00	3:20:00	3:31:00	
5:15	15:45	26:15	52:30	1:18:45	1:45:00	1:50:47	2:11:15	2:37:30	3:03:45	3:30:00	3:41:33	
5:30	16:30	27:30	55:00	1:22:30	1:50:00	1:56:03	2:17:30	2:45:00	3:12:30	3:40:00	3:52:06	
5:45	17:15	28:45	57:30	1:26:15	1:55:00	2:01:20	2:23:45	2:52:30	3:21:15	3:50:00	4:02:39	
6:00	18:00	30:00	1:00:00	1:30:00	2:00:00	2:06:36	2:30:00	3:00:00	3:30:00	4:00:00	4:13:12	
6:15	18:45	31:15	1:02:30	1:33:45	2:05:00	2:11:53	2:36:15	3:07:30	3:38:45	4:10:00	4:23:45	
6:30	19:30	32:30	1:05:00	1:37:30	2:10:00	2:17:09	2:42:30	3:15:00	3:47:30	4:20:00	4:34:18	
6:45	20:15	33:45	1:07:30	1:41:15	2:15:00	2:22:26	2:40:45	3:22:30	3:56:15	4:30:00	4:44:51	
7:00	21:00	35:00	1:10:00	1:45:00	2:20:00	2:27:42	2:55:00	3:30:00	4:05:00	4:40:00	4:55:24	
7:15	21:45	36:15	1:12:30	1:48:45	2:25:00	2:32:58	3:01:15	3:37:30	4:13:45	4:50:00	5:05:57	
7:30	22:30	37:30	1:15:00	1:52:30	2:30:00	2:38:15	3:07:30	3:45:00	4:22:30	5:00:00	5:16:30	
7:45	23:15	38:45	1:17:30	1:56:15	2:35:00	2:43:32	3:13:45	3:52:30	4:31:15	5:10:00	5:27:03	
8:00	24:00	40:00	1:20:00	2:00:00	2:40:00	2:48:48	3:20:00	4:00:00	4:40:00	5:20:00	5:37:36	
8:15	24:45	41:15	1:22:30	2:03:45	2:45:00	2:54:04	3:26:15	4:07:30	4:48:45	5:30:00	5:48:09	
8:30	25:30	42:30	1:25:00	2:07:30	2:50:00	2:59:21	3:32:30	4:15:00	4:57:30	5:40:00	5:58:42	
8:45	26:15	43:45	1:27:30	2:11:15	3:04:38	3:38:45	3:38:45	4:22:30	5:06:15	5:50:00	6:09:15	

Online Resources

Calculators

www.mcmillanrunning.com

www.runnersworld.com/tools

www.runsmartproject.com/calculator

Race Calendars/Listings

www.coolrunning.com

www.halfmarathons.net

hobbyathletes.com

www.marathonguide.com

www.runningintheusa.com

trailrunner.com

www.ultramarathonrunning.com

Training Programs

bobschul.com

www.halhigdon.com

www.jeffgalloway.com

www.mcmillanrunning.com

Clubs

www.50anddcmarathongroupusa.com

www.50statemarathonclub.com

www.50sub4.com

www.50stateshalfmarathonclub.com

www.100marathonclub.us

www.100marathonclub.org.uk

www.sevencontinentsclub.com

www.official7continentsmarathonclub.com

www.icemarathon.com

www.marathonmaniacs.com

www.halffanatics.com

www.rrca.com

trailrunner.com

Statistics

www.runningusa.org

About the Author

A lifetime runner, Robin Groves began running around the block for fun as a young child. Never one to be chosen first for teams in gym class, and usually taken last, she soon discovered that running was not only fun, but that she could literally outrun her P.E. classmates. And so her appreciation of running grew.

Robin ran her first road race at 13, the hills of cross country and ovals of track in high school and in college, and her first marathon at 19. It would be the first of 11 marathon finishes, and counting, including her long-time quest of running the Boston Marathon. She continues to run and chase new racing goals each year.

Robin earned a Bachelor of Science degree in natural science/sports medicine and a Master of Sport Science degree. She has promoted the sport of running and educated runners as a high school cross country coach, personal trainer, beginner running instructor, and by implementing and directing an elementary school running program.

Robin believes one of the best aspects of the sport of running/racing is its inclusivity. Runners and races welcome all—regardless of age, experience level and degree of ability. Runners support and inspire each other.

There are a multitude of reasons for Robin's strong affection for running—post–long run, guilt-free "Sunday Night Ice Cream Night" (it's earned!); quiet time for thought (hours and hours and hours of thought); recognizing kindred spirits by spotting their distinguishable runner's legs in any crowd, car decals, and race shirt wardrobes; instant running friends; seeing the entire age spectrum at races; our sporting events with thousands of participants; inspirational stories; and more; but most importantly, for the personal empowerment that the sport exudes. When facing tough challenges, in the sport or in everyday life, runners develop the confidence and strength to overcome them.

As much as Robin loves running, it is not her true talent. Most say her gift is organization. She has combined her passion and zeal for running and experience from decades of racing, with her organizational skills for this race results journal project.

Additional Titles

Glory Days—Cross County 4 Year Racing Journal

Glory Days—Track and Field 4 Year Results Journal